MAMMALS

HAIRY, MILK-MAKING ANIMALS

by Laura Purdie Salas   illustrated by Rosiland Solomon

Picture Window Books
Minneapolis, Minnesota

Thanks to our advisers for their expertise, research, and advice:

Robert C. Dowler, Ph.D.
Tippett Professor of Biology and Curator of Mammals
Angelo State University
San Angelo, Texas

Terry Flaherty, Ph.D., Professor of English
Minnesota State University, Mankato

Editor: Shelly Lyons
Designer: Lori Bye
Page Production: Melissa Kes
Art Director: Nathan Gassman
Editorial Director: Nick Healy
Creative Director: Joe Ewest
The illustrations in this book were created digitally and with pencil.

Picture Window Books
151 Good Counsel Drive
P.O. Box 669
Mankato, MN 56002-0669
877-845-8392
www.picturewindowbooks.com

Photo Credits: page 22 (top row, left to right, and repeated uses),
iStockphoto/Eric Isselée, Fotolia/Fernando Cerecedo, iStockphoto/
Angelika Schwarz, iStockphoto/Maxim Kulko, Shutterstock/Steffen
Foerster Photography, iStockphoto/George Peters, iStockphoto/
Eric Isselée, Shutterstock/Paul-André Belle-Isle, Shutterstock/Gregg
Williams, iStockphoto/Le Do.

Printed in the United States of America.

 All books published by Picture Window Books
are manufactured with paper containing at least
10 percent post-consumer waste.

Library of Congress Cataloging-in-Publication Data
Salas, Laura Purdie.
Mammals : hairy, milk-making animals / by Laura Purdie Salas ;
illustrated by Rosiland Solomon
p. cm. — (Amazing science. Animal classification)
Includes index.
ISBN 978-1-4048-5525-0 (library binding)
1. Mammals—Classification—Juvenile literature.
2. Mammals—Juvenile literature. I. Solomon, Rosiland, ill.
II. Title.
QL708.S25 2010
599—dc22   2009003293

Table of Contents

A World Full of Animals

Millions of animals live on our planet. Scientists classify animals, or group them together, by looking at how the animals are alike or different.

FISH

INSECT

REPTILE

AMPHIBIAN

All mammals have certain things in common: they have a backbone, they have hair or fur, they feed their young milk, they are warm-blooded, and they have lungs that take in oxygen.

Six of the more familiar main groups of animals living on Earth are: mammals, birds, reptiles, amphibians, fish, and insects. Let's take a closer look at mammals.

MAMMAL

BIRD

Bones and Hair

All mammals are vertebrates. That means they have a backbone. The backbone helps to protect an animal's spinal cord.

beluga whales

A backbone is made up of many small bones. The bones are hard enough to protect the soft spinal cord. The spinal cord contains nerves that send information to and from the brain.

Mammals also grow hair or fur on their bodies. Most mammals have coats their entire lives. Some mammals have hair only when they are young. Hair can help keep animals warm. Hair, such as a male lion's mane, can also protect an animal by making it look larger than it really is.

African lions

Live Birth

Almost all mammals give birth to live young. Newborn mammals look very similar to adult mammals. For example, a young bat looks like a smaller copy of its parents.

fruit bats

There are about 5,000 species, or kinds, of mammals. Only five species of mammals lay eggs. The five species are different kinds of platypuses and spiny anteaters. All other mammals give birth to live young.

platypus

Mammals Make Milk

All female mammals make milk for their young to drink. Newborn mammals drink their mother's milk for as long as they need to. Young elephants drink about 2.6 gallons (9.9 liters) of milk a day for four months! Then they begin eating plants. They still drink some milk until they are more than 2 years old.

Humans are mammals, too. Human babies drink only their mother's milk or milk formula until they are about 6 months old. Then they start eating solid food as well.

African elephants

Heat and Homes

All mammals are warm-blooded. That means their body temperature doesn't change much. Mammals don't need to soak up the sun's rays to warm themselves.

All mammals have lungs and need to breathe a gas called oxygen to live. Even mammals that spend a lot of time underwater need to return to the surface to take in oxygen from the air.

Because they are warm-blooded, mammals can live all around the world. They can live in freezing waters or in deserts, and everywhere in between.

river otters

Together or Alone

Wolves, giraffes, dolphins, and some other mammals live in large groups. The whole group helps to take care of the young and find food to eat. Animals that eat plants are more likely to live in groups. The group can help protect each other from enemies.

gray wolves

Grizzly bears, tigers, and some other mammals spend most of their time alone. In general, animals that eat meat are more likely to live alone. Each meat-eater needs its own hunting space.

grizzly bear

Animal groups have different names. Have you heard of a pack of wolves, a pod of dolphins, or a herd of elephants? What other animal group names do you know?

Hungry Mammals

Mammals have to eat more food than other animals of the same size. They use most of the energy they get from food to keep their bodies warm.

Not all mammals eat the same things. Some eat meat, some eat plants, and others eat both meat and plants. Dolphins, leopards, and polar bears are carnivores. They eat only meat.

porpoise: carnivore

You can tell what a mammal eats by its mouth. A carnivore usually has a wide mouth and sharp pointed teeth. An herbivore has long jaws, a long tongue, and flat teeth.

Rabbits, deer, and horses are herbivores. They eat only plants. Raccoons, pigs, and many human beings are omnivores. Omnivores eat both plants and animals.

rabbit: herbivore

raccoon: omnivore

Strange Mammals

Some mammals have unusual ways of eating. Giant anteaters slurp up ants and insects with their long snouts and sticky tongues.

giant anteater

There are mammals that eat strange things. Vampire bats drink blood. The Tasmanian devil eats mostly dead animals—even the fur and bones!

Other mammals have interesting behaviors. The jaguar is a cat that swims well! It eats fish and river otters.

jaguar

Mammals in Our World

Mammals have lived on Earth for more than 200 million years. You probably see some mammals every day.

Almost one-fourth of the world's mammal species are in danger of dying out. As we build more buildings and chop down more forests, many mammals lose their homes. Lots of people are working to help mammals survive.

Do you have a dog or a cat? It's a mammal. Maybe your classroom has a pet hamster or guinea pig. Those are mammals, too. If you see a squirrel or a rabbit outdoors, you've spotted a mammal. And of course, every time you look in the mirror, a mammal is looking back at you!

Scientific Classification Chart

The animal classification system used today was created by Carolus Linnaeus. The system works by sorting animals based on how they are alike or different.

All living things are first put into a kingdom. There are five main kingdoms. Then they are also assigned to groups within six other main headings. The headings are: phylum, class, order, family, genus, and species.

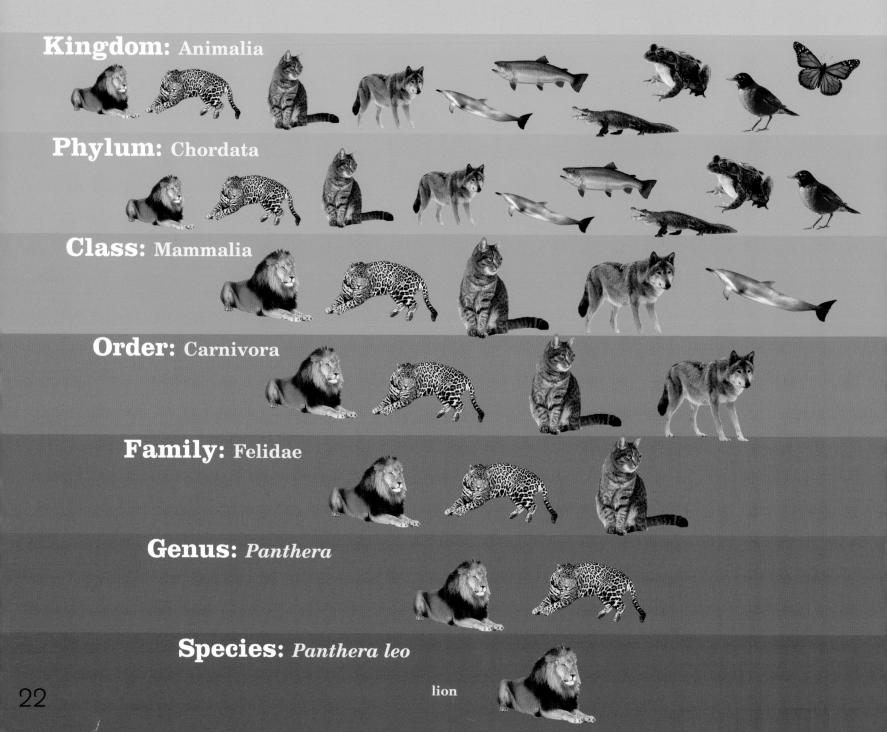

Kingdom: Animalia

Phylum: Chordata

Class: Mammalia

Order: Carnivora

Family: Felidae

Genus: *Panthera*

Species: *Panthera leo*

lion

Extreme Mammals

Largest mammal: The blue whale is the world's largest animal. It can grow to be 109 feet (33.2 meters) long and weigh 187 tons (168 metric tons).

Largest land mammal: Male African elephants can weigh 7.5 tons (6.8 metric tons). That's almost as much as an entire school bus!

Smallest mammal: The hog-nosed bat might be the smallest mammal in the world. It weighs less than a sheet of paper, and it has a wingspan of less than 6 inches (15.2 centimeters). It is also called the bumblebee bat.

Fastest land mammal: The cheetah can outrun any other land mammal. It can reach speeds of more than 70 miles (112 kilometers) per hour. This speed helps it catch other animals.

Slowest mammal: The tree sloth moves very slowly. It moves only when necessary. In fact, it could take almost 1 month for a sloth to travel just 1 mile (1.6 km)!

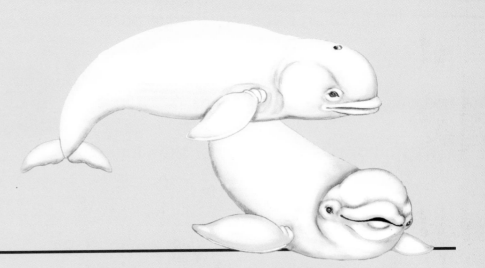

Glossary

carnivore—a meat-eating animal

coat—an animal's covering of fur or hair

herbivore—a plant-eating animal

invertebrate—an animal without a backbone

lungs—the organs in the chest that help some animals breathe

mammals—animals that have a backbone, have hair or fur, feed their young milk, are warm-blooded, and have lungs that take in oxygen

omnivore—an animal that eats both meat and plants

oxygen—a gas that people and animals must breathe to stay alive

species—a specific type of animal that has certain characteristics

vertebrate—an animal that has a backbone

warm-blooded—having a body temperature that remains the same

To Learn More

More Books to Read

Head, Honor. *Amazing Mammals*. Pleasantville, NY: Gareth Stevens Pub., 2008.

Richardson, Adele. *Mammals*. Mankato, Minn.: Capstone Press, 2005.

Walker, Sarah. *Mammals*. New York: DK Pub., 2002.

Internet Sites

FactHound offers a safe, fun way to find Internet sites related to this book. All of the sites on FactHound have been researched by our staff.

Here's all you do:

Visit *www.facthound.com*

FactHound will fetch the best sites for you!

Index

Look for all of the books in the Amazing Science: Animal Classification series:

Amphibians: Water-to-Land Animals

Birds: Winged and Feathered Animals

Fish: Finned and Gilled Animals

Insects: Six-Legged Animals

Mammals: Hairy, Milk-Making Animals

Reptiles: Scaly-Skinned Animals